I Could Just Scream

I Could Just Scream

RAY MARTINI

authorHOUSE®

AuthorHouse™ LLC
1663 Liberty Drive
Bloomington, IN 47403
www.authorhouse.com
Phone: 1-800-839-8640

Published by AuthorHouse 07/02/2014

ISBN: 978-1-4969-2401-8 (sc)
ISBN: 978-1-4969-2400-1 (e)

This Book is dedicated to my wife, Diana,

for putting up with me for 44 years.

To my friend, Oscar Sanchez,

for helping edit this book
and for being a damn good Project Manager.

Contents

Introduction

There are several social issues that need open and honest discussion in our country, but between political correctness and a general sense of apathy, you don't hear much about them. Ideally I would like to start a national dialog on them, however, that's a pretty lofty goal, so how about just a few of us clear minded people talk about them and we'll see where it goes from there. I will try to keep it interesting and informative, while not leaving anything out. But let me say from the start that I will approach these issues very candidly. You may agree, disagree, throw a fit, or whatever fires your rocket, go for it. But I will not be careful, sensitive or politically correct, so be forewarned. Ready? Here we go.

1. The English Language

Have you listened to young people speak recently? If you removed the words, "Totally Awesome", "Like"," Um','"You Know" and "Dude" from the English language, many young people would be damn near mute, which might not be a bad thing. What about "You see what I'm saying?" and "I feel you"? I'm serious. Even when college kids are interviewed on TV, it's a constant barrage of "Dude, we were like, you know, looking at this totally awesome thing, when, see what I'm saying?"....... English is a pretty good language for those people who have bothered to learn it. For those who haven't bothered, not only do you sound ignorant, but you are also limiting yourselves more that you realize.

I knew one Engineer, who could neither write nor spell very well, tell me that it was because he took only one English Class in college. I said, "Didn't you take English in High School? For that matter, isn't English your native language?" He was a pretty smart guy, but any time he had to put something in writing, it was a disaster.

Yes, I realize that each generation has it's own "cool" slang, but when we were young, we at least knew that we were speaking in slang. Today I'm not sure that people are even aware of how much they are butchering the English Language. And plenty of kids only know "street language" which really won't do them much good outside of their immediate neighborhood. In fact, they will be labeled and stereotyped the minute they open their mouths. It's really time to get better, folks. If you want to be treated like a professional, step one is to speak like one. Whether it's fair or not, you will be judged by how you speak. And don't cry about how you just want to be judged for who you really are, not just the way you speak. Lesson One; Life is not fair. Lesson Two; Life is tough, buy a helmet, DUDE. I don't care if you think it's too damn hard to learn correct English, get over it. By the way, you will also be judged by the way you dress. Wear your pants half way down around your ass and, bingo, instant gang member. Got it?

However, I must also note that some people actually learn the language a little too well. Most of those people are Politicians and those slick talking, silver tongued devils don't use the same words as we do. For example, you and I might say; "Man, I really screwed that up". But a good politician would say, **"My fellow Americans, although my office had all the best of intentions, there seems to have been a breakdown in communications somewhere and we are investigating this issue and will get to the bottom of it,**

because you, as hard working taxpayers, deserve the truth in this very important matter". Harrumph !!

OK, enough of that. But for the majority of the younger generation, English seems to be optional. Now we even have abbreviated words, which aren't supposed to be abbreviated. "He dissed me", instead of "He disrespected me". "I'm from the hood", instead of "I'm from the neighborhood". Well, maybe he like dissed you because you presented yourself as an ignoramus from the hood, Dude, you see what I'm saying?

At any rate, it is disheartening to hear English brutalized so often.

Good God, folks, it's your native language, learn it and use it. And pull your damn pants up.

So why don't our schools do a better job of teaching our native language along with the other basics?

2. Schools Don't Teach, They Preach.

A bit of an overstatement, but not as much as you might think. I have seen survey after survey showing that high school students and many college students could not even find the USA on a world map. What? Seriously, these young folks could not find their own country on the map. Now that is sad. In street interviews, many could not tell you who the President of the USA is, let alone the VP. Don't even think about their Senator or Congressman. And it was frightening that so many of them had no idea about the historical significance of the Revolutionary War, The Civil War, WW I & II.

Far too many didn't even know what country The Revolutionary War and The Civil War were fought in. That's right. They didn't know that the American Civil War was fought in America. Ask them what the national debt is and see what happens. But then ask them about the latest singer/movie star to do something stupid.

So what do these young, future leaders, know? Well, they were all pretty good at recognizing the pictures of Rap Stars, Movie Stars, and Extreme Left Wing Zealots. I guess that's something, isn't it? They will all know the latest "Social Media" device and most of them will know the quickest place to get high. Hey, just telling it like it is.

But at least our elementary schools are safe. I mean, just let some 6 year old would - be terrorist dare to point his finger like a gun and, WHAM, we call the cops, his parents, the school board and the 3rd Marine Division to stop the little hoodlum in his tracks before he can do any damage. Whew, that was a close one. I'm afraid that Political Correctness and CYA has even made in down into our Elementary Schools. Little boys have actually been accused of "Sexual Harassment" for holding a little girl's hand or kissing her on the cheek. And the so-called Adults take that seriously !! They can't manage to teach "Little Johnny" to read, but they can sure as hell brand him as a "Sexual Predator" before the poor kid even knows what that means. How stupid can you get?

My God, people, what the hell ever happened to common sense?

OK, on to higher education, maybe we will find some there.

3. College

I have always been for education, as much of it as a person can get. But education can mean, not only academia, but technical schools, trade schools, OJT and something called experience. And occasionally a person might even get an education in college, or so I'm told. I think college degrees are great; they look real pretty all framed up on the wall. The problem is that a degreed person is assumed to be educated just by virtue of his/her degree. Ever met a degreed person who had trouble getting dressed in the morning? I once had to hire a guy to drive a spare car for me to a remote project in Texas. All he had to do was follow me to the job site in the car, we would leave that car there, and he would ride back with me. Times were tough during that period in Texas so I had several guys interview for the quick one day job. One of them had a PhD in something or other. A PhD and I didn't trust him to drive a car. I don't know what planet this guy was from, and I don't know if he was on drugs or just goofy as hell, but I ended up hiring a regular guy who just plain needed a day's pay. I think Mr. PhD is still trying to find his way home.

OK, so lots of college graduates are intelligent, have some common sense, and a good sense of humor, too. I know many engineers, for example, that are real good folks. And teachers, for the most part, are not only degreed, but are some of the best people I have ever met. Doctors are special, which is why it is so bad when they go wrong. I even like lawyers. I'm more leery of them, but we do need them. And of course there is a whole host of other professions with degrees, as well. As I said, real education is great.

Therefore, real educators are great, too. After all, they are the people, from kindergarten through college and beyond, who help us reach whatever level of education we can. Well, most of them will. But the exceptions, especially on the college level, need to be identified because I'm telling you there are some professors out there do not want to educate, they want to brainwash the students. I'm talking about professors who preach such a left wing ideology, who try to indoctrinate the young people into their own radical group, that it is really frightening. There are professors that preach, rather than teach, their own agenda and not follow any kind of approved curriculum. Now, I'm all for allowing flexibility, to help students think on their own, etc., but when you condemn the entire Democratic or Capitalistic System in favor of Socialism or even Radical Islam, then it's time to step in and bring things back under control. And it's not an environment where these ideas are floated to introduce the students to them. No, it's an environment where you either accept what the Nutty Professor believes, without questions or challenges, or you don't pass the course, period. Professor Extreme Left Wing Nutcase says it's his way or the highway. Now, how do I know this? From videos, secretly filmed in classrooms across the country, even high school level, in some cases. We also see how many prominent conservative speakers are not allowed to speak on the college circuit because the extreme left wing faction refuses to listen to anyone with a different opinion than their own. And that goes for the faculty as well as the students. Those few who are invited are often heckled so badly that they are forced to leave for their own safety. This is another example of how college staff and students, our future leaders, are unwilling to even listen to another point of view. They are indoctrinated into such left wing extremism at such an early age, they are already lost. And remember, the media is filled with left wing zealots, so many of these incidents are never shown to the general public. But look around on You Tube and what you see in classrooms around the country is pretty scary. If you like what you see, if you like the brain-washing that goes on,then you probably won't like the rest of this book. But keep reading, who knows, you may even learn something.

So why don't we just get rid of these extremists? Try to fire a professor with tenure, good luck with that. The Teacher's Union has things tied up so tightly that even a criminal conviction may not allow for termination. Suspension with pay, if that, is the norm. In my book, no pun intended, that's called a paid vacation. So colleges and universities take the easy way out and don't confront these loons. And it's the students who suffer for it. They may not realize it at the time, but the students really are the long term losers because they never learn how to look at both sides of an issue before making up their minds. They are shown only one way to think and many of them will carry that narrow minded perspective into adulthood and into whatever profession they choose.

It is not overly dramatic to say that that closed minded way of thinking is how the government controls the people in places like North Korea and Iran. Try expressing your own thoughts in those countries and see what happens to you. We have a Constitutional Right to Free Speech and Expression in this country. But those are like muscles; if you don't use them, they will weaken. Got your attention, yet?

As an aside, I think that name brand colleges (Ivy League Schools, for example) are the most overrated items on a resume. I have seen hundreds of engineers and management folks hired, fired, promoted, etc., but I really can't think of many cases at all where those things were done based on the name brand college that that person attended. Bosses hire/promote people because they want someone who can do the job, period. Yes, I know there are exceptions, but generally speaking, the boss wants someone who can handle the job regardless of the college that person attended. Now there is always the local favorite school, of course. If you graduated from the same school as the person interviewing you, that can be a big advantage. But that can apply to literally any school, big or small, in the country. For my money, pick a good state college or university, study hard and you should do as well as someone who paid 5 times what you did for their name brand education. And hopefully you won't have to start your career with a crushing student loan to be paid back.

But that's academia. What about the social side?

4. Social Skills Lost.

When I was a kid, about 100 years ago, we played outside whenever it wasn't raining or dark. We wanted to be outside and our parents wanted us to be outside. And I think that was a very good thing to be, outside that is. I say that because when we were outside, we were either playing some type of ballgame, or riding our bikes, or running around the neighborhood causing minor problems. What we were not doing is sitting in front of the TV, or the computer screen or poking away at some other form of inanimate electronic device, like an I Phone, I Pad or Cell Phone, etc. Now one reason for that was because most of those things, except the TV, hadn't been invented yet. But regardless, what we were doing was "Socializing" with real live people. We learned how to get along with other kids, older and younger. Sure we'd fight at times, but we'd get over it, too. And that was all part of our street education, so to speak.

Yes, we had TV, the baby boomer generation was the first to grow up with it. But TV was something to watch after supper, after the street lights came on and we were in for the night. But right after school, and certainly on the weekends, the last thing we wanted was to be stuck at home. There was baseball, football, wiffle ball and stick ball to be enjoyed. Later, into my teens, I even discovered girls. Wow. They were better than wiffle ball, but a lot harder to understand.

Or just hanging around with the guys was great. Even as kids, we were much more comfortable with our peers than we were alone and isolated. Have you seen teenagers walking around today? Even when there are several of them together, they are often alone with their electronic devices, at least in their own minds. I've seen a group of friends walking along in the mall, each one of them talking/tweeting to other friends on their I phones. I think the term for that is Stovepiping, meaning their focus is isolated from the people right next to them. I have another word for it, Sad. So what are the kids saying to each other anyway? Most of the time, NOT MUCH. When they tweet, they tell other kids that they are walking around the mall, that they are in school or some other mundane activity that no one is really interested in anyway. Even on Facebook, I see entries all the time that say, "I'm at work" or "I'm at the gym". So what? I think what people are really saying is; "Hey, here I am, recognize me. I am a real person with feelings and I really need someone to respond to me so that I feel validated."

But that would be too humiliating to say out loud, so they say "I'm at work".

Plus I don't believe most young people read the newspaper or listen to the news to find out what's going on in the world anyway, so they stay blissfully ignorant chatting away on their electronic devices. Although in their defense, much of the news media is questionable, as we'll see in the next chapter. But kids, take a hint. Put that damn device away and talk to your friends, you might even get to like them.

5. The News Media: Are You People Serious?

Let's get in my time machine and return to the 1950's and 60's. Not to worry, I promise to bring you back, for a small fee. Back in the dark ages when I was growing up, we had TV with the usual amount of fluff like Game Shows, Soap Operas, Westerns, Variety Shows and then something called The News Hour. The News Hour was just that; at 6PM the local news, sports and weather would come on for a 1/2 hour, followed by national & world news, sports and weather for another 1/2 hour. That was it. Then it went back to regular programming, good and bad. For that short period of time, news people would give the major events of the day, in town and then across the country. They would give you the facts. They were news people. They did not, almost without exception, give you their own political or social viewpoint. That would never fly. As an example, at one point in TV history, an anchorman named Walter Cronkite was known as the most trusted man in America. He worked for CBS News for decades and was the Number One Go-To Guy for the straight scoop. He was the guy who made the announcement that JFK had been assassinated. Well, 'Ol Walter was one of the most Liberal, Left Wing Newscasters on TV, but almost NONE of the viewers knew it. Why? Because Walter knew it was his job to give the news, the facts, and not try to use his influence by spinning the news to serve his personal ideology.

Of course that was when there were only the three major news outlets: ABC, NBC and CBS. Now we have cable and we are *blessed* with 100's of channels of junk to watch. And the news? Objective? Factual? Well, not so much. 'Ol Walter would turn over in his grave.

Before I go any further, let me say that my purpose here is NOT to take sides politically, but only to point out the bias that permeates the news business. Bear with me, please.

So let's return in our time machine to modern day news coverage. ABC, NBC and CBS are overtly and blatantly Left Wing Liberals and they don't even try to hide it. Wow, I can hear the roar of the Lefties defending their boys. Save it, anyone who is even the least bit objective knows it's true. Anyway, what they call news is not much more than cheerleading for the Democratic Party, regardless of the facts. Take any given story, apply the Liberal Spin and present it to the public.

And always follow these rules.

1. Minimize anything negative about the Liberal Democrats.

2. Maximize anything negative about the Conservative Republicans.

3. When you can not spin a damaging story far enough about the Liberals, don't run it at all. And when there is a negative story about the Conservatives, run it to death.

Think I'm exaggerating? Remember Benghazi where Four Americans died and the Obama Administration lied about some video being the cause? If you only watched Main Street Media you might have missed it since it wasn't covered for very long. But what about the traffic jam in New Jersey under Republican Governor Christie? Even though there was never any evidence of his involvement, the media ran that story to death. Americans killed; not important. Traffic jam; run with it. The same thing happened with Fast & Furious; NSA Scandal; and the IRS Scandal. Don't recognize these? That's because they all showed the Democrats in a bad light, so the Main Street Media showed very little coverage, if at all.

Now, with cable of course, there are a number of news outlets beyond the original three. Take MSNBC, which is owned by NBC. I actually force myself to watch MSNBC, occasionally, just to get all sides of an issue, but those people need some serious help.

I won't mention anyone by name, but the dribble they substitute for news is ridiculous.

Professionalism, objectivity, and even just basic facts don't stand a chance on that network. This is the show where one of their anchormen described how he felt when he listened to an Obama speech. He would actually get chills up and down his leg. Good God. Real hard hitting journalism there, eh? Oh, the same guy once described Obama as "The Perfect American". Now is that news or cheer-leading?

Give me a break, Look, whether you are a Democrat, Republican, Independent, Libertarian or anything else, you should demand that news organizations are unbiased and give you the straight scoop. Otherwise, you might as well be watching State Sponsored TV, much like North Korea or Iran, where the government decides what you will watch. Pitiful.

By the way, as more and more people catch on, MSNBC's rating are plummeting and understandably so.

Speaking of network news, have you seen the buffoonery that goes on in the typical network morning shows? There are usually 4 or 5 people sitting at a desk, all dressed up pretty with million dollar smiles, laughing, giggling, teasing each other and drinking coffee. Well, that's all well and good, BUT, they are supposed to be doing the news !! Instead we get to hear all about their weekend and who did what, and look how cute someone's dog is. Then, if you suffer through that, you get force fed an Obama Sandwich, like it or not.

They are not exactly "hard-hitting" investigative journalists. They are unprofessional moronic, grinning sycophants, who have no idea what both sides of an issue look like. They just read the teleprompter, deliver the message and follow the Left Wing Script.

And the script is rather predictable. Pro Liberal, Anti-Conservative and look how cute my dog is.

OK, so what about the Conservative Networks? Actually there is only one that I know of, and that's FOX News. FOX, whether you like them or not, is the clear leader in ratings of all cable news networks. That's a fact. Now I know many people who just hate FOX News. Fine, no problem. Everyone is entitled to their own opinion. But the thing I find interesting is when you ask many of them just what it is that they don't like, they will tell you that FOX is very biased and is all for the Republicans. OK, still no problem. That's not true, but fine, so far. But then I ask them to give me an example.. That's when it gets interesting because they will finally admit that they have never watched it. "Hell No", most of them tell me. "I'm not going to watch those liars." Hmmm. So you hate a network that you've never watched. That usually puts them on defensive. What they are saying is that they hate FOX News because the liberal media told them that they should hate FOX News. Now they will never admit that, in so many words, but how else do you explain hating a TV network that you've never seen?

At least I watch MSNBC. I hate it, but I hate it because I've watched it and it is just so much dribble, not because I was told to hate it. I also watch CNN, which can run hot and cold, so I'll leave them alone. But the 3 major TV networks and MSNBC are bad, real bad.

Also The Good Reverend Al is on MSNBC. Now there is a piece of work, I tell you. And the one thing you will always hear from him and others on MSNBC is how bad racism is in our country, over and over. That's how he makes his living; pumping all the racist hate speech he can muster up and criticizing FOX News. And yet while spewing all the racist hate speech, I've seen this guy stumble over more words reading the teleprompter than a 4 year old just learning to read. What a guy.

Now, in all honesty, I'm not saying that FOX News is always perfectly objective. I guess no station is, but it's a matter of degrees. So the critics can say, "Well both sides are biased." OK, but the point is whether you lean right or fall left. Hey, I like that !

However, the general public is largely to blame. Just like we get the government we deserve, we get the media we allow to exist. The main street media has sold out to the liberals and there is no public outcry.

Anytime there are no serious consequences, nothing will change. Yup, we let it happen, but we can fix it, if we really want to.

I mentioned racist hate speech, so let's look further into that. I warn you, again, I pull no punches. So put on your thick skin or forever hold your hurt feelings. Certainly this is only my humble opinion, but keep an open mind and I think you will see lots of things you recognize.

6. Racism is Upside Down

Touchy subject, but why stop now?

If you ask most people, black or white, whether or not racism still exists, I think you would get a majority of them to say yes. Maybe not as bad as it used to be, but it is still around. OK, I agree. But they are talking about white people being racist against black people. OK, I still agree. But what if you phrased the question differently? What if you said, "Are some black people racist, too?" "Are there black people who do not like white people just because they are white"? Try it sometime and you will get a confused look from people. And it is understandable because of our cultural history. Look, we all know about slavery, Jim Crow Laws, The KKK, and lynching of black men.

All of that is well documented and I certainly don't mean to minimize any of it. But slavery is gone, Jim Crow Laws are gone, the KKK is all but gone and we don't lynch black men anymore. So what was the next step? Well, things moved on to The Civil Rights Movement, Affirmative Action, etc., and things got much better than they had been. Yes, that's right, things are much better than they had been, despite what certain factions of the black community keep telling us in order to promote racial division. Why? Because that's how they make their living. Racism is a cash crop and it is very profitable. Those hate mongers don't want to work on solutions to current problems. Hell no, if they solved the problem, they would be out of work. So they keep pumping all the hate and vitriol they can into everything they say and do, and Political Correctness will prevent most people from arguing back. Let me be clear, many black leaders do not want racism to go away, they thrive on it and do whatever they can to perpetuate it.

So what about black racism? When do you ever hear any news commentator, black or white, talking about black on white crime? Look at the statistics and you will see that black on black crime is the most prevalent. Black on White crime is next and White on Black crime is a very distant third. But what makes the news? What gets the president of the US on TV talking about racism? That's right, White on Black. Need some examples? Remember Trayvon Martin who was black, and George Zimmerman who is white? Best evidence showed that Trayvon was beating Zimmerman when Zimmerman shot him in Self Defense. You may not want to hear that, but that's a fact. If you watched the trial with an open mind, you really couldn't come away with any other verdict. However, if you thought that Zimmerman was guilty just because he is white, then no amount of evidence will convince you otherwise. But the jury got it right and, in fact, the case should never have gone to trial in the first place. At any rate, that didn't stop the president from going on national TV and telling the world that if he, Obama, had a son, that son would look like Trayvon Martin. Nothing prejudicial there.

What Crap ! Can you imagine if George W Bush were president and made a similar statement about Zimmerman? The Main Street Media would have gone ballistic. But not a word about a blatantly racist comment, meant to prejudice the case, was ever said.

So what about Black on White crime committed every day in many cities throughout the country? See much in the papers or on TV? Not a chance. Ever heard Obama condemn black on white crime? Nope. Oh sure, he talks about all crime and all racism being a bad thing, but he only points out the individual cases where the white guy is accused of a crime against the black guy. Remember the Beer Summit? In 2009 a black man was arrested by a white cop in Massachusetts. No big thing, strictly a local case. But Obama immediately got on TV and said that even though he didn't know all the facts, he thought that the white cop overreacted. Even though he didn't know all the facts !! And why the hell is he sticking his nose into local police business anyway? So then both the black guy and the white cop were invited to the white house for the Beer Summit where they talked it all out and held hands and wasn't that nice.

This was a clear cut case of pandering to the Black Constituency and Obama did it shamelessly. Frankly, the Black Community should have seen it for what it really was and acted accordingly. Even Joe Biden was there. Good God.

How much did that farce cost the taxpayer? **And the liberal press never said a word.**

We have racism in this country because some people, black and white, are ignorant and narrow minded. That's a given. But fueling the fire is the one sided media and several black public figures who take advantage of the situation for their own financial and political gain.

The real litmus test on this issue is to reverse the circumstances in some of the cases and see what would happen. I gave the example earlier of a white president saying that if he had a son, he would look like George Zimmerman and what a PR disaster that would be. But there are several more. Remember Ray Nagin, the Black Democratic Mayor of New Orleans during hurricane Katrina? The Honorable Mayor Nagin, in speaking about rebuilding the city after the storm, said that his city should be a "Chocolate City", meaning that he wanted it populated mainly by black people. He actually said that on national TV and the liberal media ignored it. So again, turn it around and have a white mayor say that he wants a "Vanilla City" and see what happens.

By the way, The Former Honorable Mayor Nagin has since been convicted of taking bribes, fraud, etc, and will be sentenced to prison. And when the media gave the news about his conviction, all they reported was that the Former Mayor of New Orleans was convicted, and so on. Not one of them mentioned the word Democrat. And the story was shown, then dropped. But when reporting about the New Jersey Traffic Jam, it was always, The Republican Governor, etc.

OK, but those are individuals. What about organizations? Are there organizations that are blatantly racist? Well, for starters:

A. The NAACP, The National Association for the Advancement of Colored People.

   Try starting a National Association for White People, see what happens.

B. The Black Caucus

   What about a White Caucus?

C. Black Miss America Pageant, open to only black women

   Black women can compete in the Miss American pageant, but white woman can not compete in the Black Miss America Pageant.

D. The United Negro College Fund

E. The National Association of Black Journalists

F. The National Black MBA Association

G. The National Association of Black Hotel Owners

H. The National Association of Black Accountants.

I. 100 Black Men of America

J. The Association of Black Psychologists

That's just ten and there are many more. Do an internet search for Black Organizations and see just how many there are. So the point is this; if it's all about racial equality, then why can't white people have similar organizations? Because it's not about equality. It's about having your cake and eating it, too. Don't you dare tell a black man or woman that they can't join something, you racist bastard. But you damn well better leave black people alone to start their own thing and exclude you just because you are white. And don't you dare object either, you racist bastard. Is that equality? Did I mention that you are a racist bastard?

But understand, the truth is that I am very much in favor of any group being able to organize based on whatever demographic they happen to be. As long as it's not violent or some nut case group, then go for it.

So it's fine by me if we have Jewish Organizations, Women's Groups, Senior Citizen's Clubs, Girl Scouts, Boy's Club and Hispanic Groups.

And I certainly have no problem with organizations that black people want to form, with the possible exception of the Black Panthers, who are a little too militant for me.

But why is it that as soon as you put the word White in front of any organization, Oh No, you can't do that, that's a bad thing? How can you even say that? Shut it down !!

If it's OK for Black People, Women, Jews, Hispanics, Boys and Girls, why not just plain 'ol White People? I want to start the White Older Guys Society, better know as WOGS. Sounds pretty harmless to me. WOGS of the world unite !!

It's just so wasteful, all of it. What if we left out the words Black and White and just substituted the word People? Just plain People. Naw, that would never work, would it?

So that's why the title of this chapter is Racism is Up Side Down. I could just have well entitled it Racism is Just So Stupid. Which brings me to the next subject, old age. What's the connection, you may ask? I'll get back to you on that.

7. Old Age - Golden Years

OK, let's change the subject. I am now called a Senior Citizen, among other things.

I am a baby boomer, actually the start of the baby boomers, since I was born in 1946. If you read my previous book, and shame on you if you didn't - it's called "*The Death of Leadership*", available on Amazon and Barnes & Noble, then you know how I worked for 47 years, retired, and wrote the book about how much things have changed in business and politics. Yes, I know, that was shameless Self-Promotion. So What?

Well, other things have changed, too, like my body, my strength and my perspective.

I just had cataract surgery in both eyes and I see much better, thank you. I've also had some back problems and a bit of arthritis, but nothing too serious. But bad enough for doctors to say things like "Well, Mr Martini, you have to realize that as we get older........". WE? You little bastard, you are only 35, I think to myself. I don't say it out loud because he has some sharp medical implement in his hand and I'm not stupid. Old yes, but not stupid.

I used to love to play baseball, softball, football, stick ball, wiffle ball, etc., when I was younger. I rode motorcycles for years until my right hand, throttle hand, started to go numb. Oh yea, and I have now made out my final will and testament. I also gave my doctor a thing called "Instructions to Doctor" which tells him not go to any extraordinary means to keep me alive should things really go south. It's called a DNR, meaning "Do Not Resuscitate". I have also put on a few pounds over the years. Don't ask, it's none of your business. Geeesh.

On the other hand, I really can't complain. Many people my age and younger have some serious medical problems and some didn't even make it to 67. So I'm whining just a little, but I realize I'm pretty lucky, too. Hell, I can still eat just about anything I want, have a glass of wine occasionally and play some poker at the casino, so life is really pretty good . . . .today. Check back with me tomorrow.

But there is one inescapable fact that can not be denied. On balance, old age sucks and things ain't gonna get no better. I know, the English ain't so great in that sentence. Um, it's like some totally awesome poetic license, Dude. Sorry about that. Anyway, one way old age can be perceived is by the number of things I probably will never do again. Now in some cases that's good, in other cases, not so much. Things like Motorcycle Riding; Softball; Getting into a Bar Fight or even Getting Drunk are gone. Since I've been married almost 44 years, I think I can rule out ever doing those things again. So that's just another way to keep score, so to speak. Anyway, the fact is that every day I wake up is another day I get to live and that's a good thing. However, it is also another day closer to my demise.

I think of life as a long conveyor belt. Some people fall off early, some stay on later, but eventually everyone comes to the end. Wow, that is pretty depressing, maybe I'll take that part out. Naw, what the hell.

I think it was some old codger who came up with the name "The Golden Years". He is probably the same guy who had a dog with only 3 legs, just one ear and was blind in one eye. Yup, he named his dog "Lucky".

And my perspective is getting older, too, so to speak. I see things differently now than when I was young, as I'm sure most people do. In fact, if you have the same opinions at my age that you had at the age of 21, it means you probably haven't learned much in all those years. Of course we see things differently and our priorities change. When I drive down the road, I could care less if someone wants to pass me. I just move over and let them go by. At one time, there was no way in hell anyone was going to pass me on the road, forget about it.

I know that's a minor thing, and there are lots of other things that seemed to be absolutely critical when I was younger, but now seem pretty silly. Is my hair combed just right, how do my jeans fit, am I using the coolest lingo, etc.?

But other issues have replaced those type of things. I'm very concerned about future generations, for example. Hell, when I was the future generation, I couldn't have cared less, but I sure do now. I'm told that the generation behind me is the first one not to do better than the one before it. For years, most children did better than their parents and that's what built this country up to be the world leader by the end of WWII. In less than 200 years, this country went from a colony to the strongest country in the world. We have lost a lot of that and future generations are letting it slip away. How sad.

I worry about schools being slowly turned into nationally controlled cookie cutter student factories where all kids are the same and they only learn what the central government wants them to know, as I addressed in an earlier chapter.

I worry about our entitlement society reaching a tipping point from which we will not be able to return, when the "norm" is for the government to supply all that it thinks the people need and the people do only what the government thinks they should.

I worry about other countries, who hate us and would love nothing better than to see us destroyed,obtaining the very weapons it would take to accomplish that.

I worry if we will ever get our industrial base back in this country. At one time we were the leader of the entire world in manufacturing, steel, cars, consumer goods, etc. Now much of that has gone to foreign countries and millions of jobs along with it.

This country was built on capitalism, and even with all its faults and shortcomings, it's still the most effective and productive economic system ever invented. People could, and did, advance upwards and each generation was better off than the previous one. But now capitalism is a dirty word to many people. Yes, they see the abuses, but they choose to ignore the benefits. There is no question that a few people will get filthy rich, but then in my long career, no poor person ever offered me a job. Of course it isn't perfect, but the benefits far outweigh the negatives.

If you disagree, show me an economic system that has worked better then capitalism over time.

However, capitalism runs on money and the confidence we all need to have in it. Screw up the money and you will poison the well. So let's talk about money.

8. Money or Just Paper?

Got any money in your pocket? Most people would say yea, I got a few bucks, but they would be wrong. What they have are pretty pieces of colored paper that are traded for goods and services on blind faith, nothing more. You accept those pieces of paper because you can use them to buy food and other things. But the paper itself it worthless. That's right, worthless. It's called FIAT money.

FIAT money is simply paper that the government says has a certain value. So most people accept that and think of the paper itself as valuable. But remember that those pieces of paper were once backed up by gold and silver, which is real money. But those metals were cumbersome for day to day trade, so they went to more convenient paper money which represented the gold and silver. It was understood that it wasn't the paper that had value, but only the metals which backed up the paper. In fact, you could go to the bank and exchange the paper for gold. But those days are gone. When Nixon took us off the gold standard in 1971, there was only the paper left. Think about that. The paper used to be for convenience, now it is all that's left. That is Fiat Money. So now, without anything backing up the paper, the government was free to print as much of the pretty stuff as it wanted to. And did they ever. Trillions and Trillions of US Dollars were created out of thin air. The paper you carry around in your wallet or purse is useless because it has no intrinsic value.

Let's be clear. If the US Government wanted to print toilet paper with Santa Clause on it and call it money, it would have just as much intrinsic value as our dollar bills ! Think about that. The paper we carry around in our pocket is as worthless as toilet paper, and yet it is how most of us define our wealth.

So what does the US do with all this FIAT money?

For now, anyway, the US Dollar is still the currency for world trade. If any country wants to buy oil, they must do it in US Dollars. Before WW II, Great Britain was king and the British Pound was the world currency. Now it's our turn and what a deal. We can print as much of the world's currency that we want. Sounds too good to be true? Well, it is. Right now, as of 2014, we are printing Billions of US Dollars every month, which puts lots of cash into circulation and keeps the stock market going. But those dollars are literally printed out of thin air and that can not continue without consequences. It is also putting pressure on inflation, lots of pressure. You just can't keep printing paper and not expect inflation to skyrocket eventually. And when it does hit, watch out. We are not immune to hyperinflation, just like other countries have suffered. When you hear stories about people pushing wheelbarrows of cash to the store to buy bread, that's a fact. There are some currencies where the smallest denomination of paper money is in the millions. Imagine buying a loaf of bread for $25 Million Dollars. It has happened before.

There is no free lunch or free money and we will eventually pay the price, literally.

Something else, too. What happens if the US Dollar is no longer the world currency? Remember that China has been financing this country for years and they also see the pending inflation danger which may hurt all the bonds they own. They also see our skyrocketing debt. China is not stupid. They will do whatever it takes to protect themselves. And if that means that the USA suffers because of it, so what? China will protect China, period. Throw in Japan, India and others and then you realize that the USA, once the most powerful country in the world, is now very vulnerable financially on a global scale. There is no law that says that only the US Dollar must be the world currency.

What if the international banking gurus decided to let the Chinese Juan take over as world currency? Then we must buy the Chinese currency in order to do business internationally. And guess who sets the price of the Chinese Juan. And guess who the balance of power switches to for the next few generations. Speak any Chinese? *Your children will.* This is pretty serious stuff and I suggest you do your own research on it. History shows us that with the combination of stifling debt, bad monetary policy and the general entitlement mentality, no nation can survive forever. Democracies, throughout history, have lasted only from about 200 to 230 years for just those reasons. Guess how old the USA is.

I know, it's pretty heavy stuff. So let's take a break onto something not quite so serious.

9. Reality TV - Really?

OK, a little lighter subject now; lighter, sillier and dumber. Reality TV appeared out of nowhere several years ago and we still use the term as if it had some truth to it.

C'mon now, you may enjoy the shows, but reality is a bit of a stretch. I won't spend much time on this, but here are a few examples:

One show, in Detroit, shows a pawn shop which spends as much time throwing people out of their store as it does actually doing business. It was mildly entertaining the first few times I watched it, but not so much anymore. The only real part is the money those guys are making from producing the show.

Then there are shows, in no particular order, which show swamp people wrestling with alligators, people fighting to repossess cars, loggers fighting with each other in the water and truckers who continue to drive on icy roads which they say are too dangerous to drive on. Oh and don't forget the survivor shows, where people are isolated in a strange and dangerous location to fend for themselves or die. Oh My God !! Makes you wonder how the camera crew, lighting crew, sound crew, hair and makeup people, prop guys and the director survive, doesn't it? After all, they are in the same situation as the contestants. Just gives me the chills.

So why are these shows so popular? Well, for one thing, they are cheap to produce. That's right, dirt cheap. Look, when you have a show with no writers, no high paid stars in the cast and no expensive sets to build, of course it's cheap. Add to that the public's appetite for silliness on the air and you have a hit on your hands.

Now, don't get me wrong. I am a capitalist, through and through, so if it sells, what the hell, go for it. If you are entertained, fine. But even wrestling now calls itself sports entertainment, with the emphasis on entertainment. Maybe they should call it Reality Wrestling?

Now right up there with Reality TV are Reality Commercials. I can see you rolling your eyes already. Stop that, it's rude. Don't be rude, that's my job.

OK, let's be adult about this for a minute. The average commercial is childish, stupid and immature. And those are the good ones. I'm no marketing guy, but it seems to me that the average commercial is targeted towards a 12 year old mentality. I hope you're not insulted, but it's true. And the commercials which are locally done are worse yet. They try to be cute and funny, but end up being moronic. By the way, commercial makers, keep the kids out of it. Having your darling little 6 year old daughter tell me that I should take my car to her daddy for repairs, really doesn't carry much weight with me.

We have several car dealerships that advertise locally, as does everyone else, and they use the owner and/or the employees to sell us the "great deal of the day" Look, most of us really don't like car salesmen even when we have are forced to deal with them. We sure as hell don't want them in our face when we are at home. Geesh.

There is a local pharmacy in my town that runs an add where the employees wear false beards, trying to look like the Duck Dynasty Folks. I just shook my head when I saw it. Apparently someone told them that if they put false beards on...... that everyone would trust them with their medication. Just makes you wonder.

Noted Exceptions: The Hump Day Camel and the Duck. Love those guys.

OK, back to serious stuff.

10. Service Industry

Once again I jump in my Time Machine and go back to the 1950's. Picture this: You pull your car into a gas station and drive up to the pump. For one thing, gas was about 25 Cents a Gallon, but besides that, an attendant comes out and asks you what you would like. You say, "give me $2.00 worth". Hell, there were times when people would say "give me 75 cents worth". Didn't matter, whatever amount of gas you wanted, the attendant would not only pump the gas himself, but clean the windshield, check the oil and the tire pressure, if you wanted him to. That's right, you could just sit in your car and the gas station guy would do all the work. Also if you needed some work done on your car, you just pulled it into the service bay and they had a mechanic to take care of it. Anyone seen that lately? If you are under 40 years old, you may not remember that, but it was the norm, not the exception. Now that was service.

OK, back to the present. First, you pump your own gas at about $3.50 per gallon, clean your own windshield and check your own oil. Try asking the clerk at the convenience store to check your tire pressure. They will probably call the cops on you for being insane. Besides, most of the kids working there wouldn't know how to check tire pressure anyway.

OK, what about other retail outlets? Walk into most stores and ask the clerk if they have a certain item; that is if you can find a clerk in the first place. They are few and far between, usually on break and/or shooting the breeze with the other clerks. But if you are fortunate enough to get one of them to talk to you, it probably won't help much. "Excuse me, Miss, do you have any so and so here"? "Well, I, like, don't think so". "Um, well, I dunno, let me check with someone else" "Never mind, bye."

I once walked into a retail store and the only employee I saw was a girl on her cell phone. She looked up at me, then went back to her phone. After I stood there staring at her, she finally put the phone down and just looked at me. I asked her if she had any (whatever the hell I was looking for). She picked up her phone again while saying, "If we have any, it's back there ... somewhere". Unbelievable. "Never mind, bye."

But, by far, this is my favorite story. I bought a replacement cartridge for my desktop printer, took it back to the office and installed it. Well, it turns out it was defective, so I packaged it up, along with my receipt, and returned it to the store (National Chain). Well the girl at the service counter calls someone over to help me and I explain the problem to this another woman. She looks at the package and tells me I can not return it because I have opened the inner foil package that the cartridge comes in. I asked her how I was supposed to install it in the printer if I didn't take it out of the foil. She informed me that if I had only opened the outer cardboard box and NOT the foil, I could have returned it. I said that doesn't make any sense. If I didn't open the foil, how would I have known it is bad? And for God's sake, why would I buy a product, not open the inner package and then bring it back? She didn't have an answer and really didn't seem to care. OK, enough of this nonsense. I asked to see the manager. She got all puffed up and indignant and informed me that she WAS the manager, SIR ! I said "Good, then let me talk to your boss". She stomped off without another word. A few minutes later the first girl at the counter called me over and with a distinct smile on her face, issued me a refund. Mind you, this is a national chain, a BIG national chain. True Story !

I have walked out of many stores just because of the lack of courtesy and knowledge on the part of the clerks. And the thing is, many of those clerks are young people working part time, paying for school, etc., so they don't know any better unless they are taught by someone. Hello, can you say Manager??

Have you ever walked out of a restaurant due to bad service? Oh yes, I certainly have, many times. A typical scenario: My wife and I walk into a restaurant and, fairly quickly, we are seated and told that the waitress will be right with us. Mind you, we like to eat early, so the crowd really hasn't arrived yet. Anyway, we sit and wait. Meanwhile we can see 2 or 3 waitresses standing around shooting the bull and ignoring us. Well, when we see that, the clock starts ticking. They then have about 2 minutes to get to our table or we get up and leave. The same thing applies if we actually get our menus and have to wait an unreasonable amount of time for them to take our order. Now, I realize that if the place is packed, it takes longer for them to serve everyone. OK, that's fine, up to a point. I will usually give them a little extra time. But remember, if we are talking about Friday or Saturday Night Dinner Hour, why hasn't the manager anticipated the crowd and increased the crew?

But the one thing that really sets me off is when you have to wait for the check. That is ridiculous. Why would a business make you wait to pay them? For one thing, I assume they want the table for the next customer and they should also want their money. The worst thing about having to wait to pay is that you can't walk out !! But it will be a long time before I come back. Bad Service all the way around. Again, where is the management?

Speaking of bad management, let's discuss one of the poorest managed policies in our country.

11. What Immigration Policy?

OK, big switch in subject matter here.

First, I believe that Congress has the lowest approval rating that it has ever had since such things were tracked. Some polls have it as low as 10%. That is horrible, but well deserved.

What entity can sustain itself when only 10% of the people who pay for it, approve of it?

And that is not a partisan remark. It's not the Democrats or Republicans, it's the Congress as an institution.

The president, who shall remain nameless, has a higher rating, but it too has been falling steadily since he was elected. Again, well deserved.

So now we come to our National Immigration Policy, which is.......? Anybody?

No, I don't know either. We have thousands of written pages on the subject, somewhere, I'm sure, but does anyone know what the policy really is? If the policy is to keep illegal aliens out of our country, then we are not doing a very good job of it. If the policy is to let them in, give them jobs, school lunches, cell phones, an education, a welfare card, driver's license and protection, then we are doing a whale of a job. You think I'm exaggerating? Every one of those items is provided to illegal, ooops, sorry, the politically correct word now is "undocumented persons" who are in our country. And if you object to any of it, then you are branded a racist. Yup, you are a racist if you believe that we have the right and the responsibility to protect ourselves from people sneaking into our country. For the record, try sneaking into any other country and see what happens. Seriously, you will, at the very least, go to jail, if not shot on sight. But not the USA, oh no, we're the good guys, the compassionate guys, The Chumps. The rest of the world is laughing at us for being so gullible as to believe that the only people who sneak into the US A are good, honest, hardworking people who just want to support their families.

Bullshit !

Even for those that fit that category, their first official act is to break our laws rather than go through the process of legal immigration. They just don't want to have to wait their turn.

And that's the best of the crowd. Does anyone not know that there are drug smugglers, criminals, murderers, and TERRORISTS coming in with them? Wake up !! If you were a terrorist wanting to sneak into this country with minimum risk, how would you do it? The US/Mexican Border, of course.

But our government really doesn't care about that. So why does the government allow this farce to continue? Votes ! Votes ! Both parties understand that the Hispanic Population is now so large that neither side can afford to offend them by being tough on Immigration. So the flood of illegals continues and the votes continue to go to whomever is more lenient concerning Immigration. At some point, we will reach the tipping point where Hispanics will be so influential that no one will be able to reverse the trend. Actually we may already be there. That's right, we may have already lost our country, and that is a damned shame. By the way, for those of you who will jump up and yell racism, Anti-Hispanic and so forth, stuff it. I am Pro-American, first. I am not against any other nationality, but I believe we have the right and the responsibility to let only those people into our country that can contribute to the general well being, and not suck the resources dry. I also believe that we have the right to balance the immigration flow from different countries so that no one culture will rule over any other. And most importantly, no other culture will rule over our own.

If that makes me a racist, so be it. If that makes me a racist, I think we need more racists in this country. Of course I am not a racist, but I will not be intimidated into backing down just because some Bozo calls me one. There are people who are constantly attacking others by using the term 'Racist' as a hammer. Whether they are talking about Black People or Hispanic People or anyone else, the first weapon they use is to brand people "Racist".

Think about this. It's the person who sees racism everywhere they look who is the real Racist. Regardless of the situation, if all you see is Black and White, Hispanic and White, etc., then you are one who is the real racist and you attack everyone else to put other people on the defensive. Shine the harsh light of "Racism" on everyone else and hope that no one will see you for what you really are, which is an Opportunist, a Phony, a Coward and the Real Racist.

Very simply put, I am a Patriot. I want to protect this country and if you have some other agenda, then we will have a problem.

Sound a little harsh? I certainly hope so. OK, I'll try to be a bit more Civil in the next chapter.

12. Civility Lost

Now here is something we should all be concerned with because civility, or rather the lack thereof, is at a dangerous and deadly level. Look at the case of the sports fan that was beaten into a coma. Why? Because he cheered for the other team or wore their name on his jersey. What the hell is that?

Or someone who has their life threatened because they publicly voiced an opinion. By the way, it is usually the conservative opinion that stirs up all this hate from the liberals. Hell there was one case where the programming director of some TV station received threatening letters and phone calls because he changed the time slot of some program !!

Then there's road rage, where some guy wants to run you off the road or even shoots you because you weren't going fast enough for his liking.

Over and over, we see on the news where someone goes into a school, office building or restaurant and kills people indiscriminately. Most of them eventually shoot themselves before they can be arrested or they get shot by the cops. Here's a suggestion to would-be shooters: Reverse the order of things. That's right, shoot yourself first, then we'll discuss the other people later.

Where is this all coming from? Is this our future? Will we digress into a society of "shoot first, before the other guy does" mentality? I'm all for the right to own guns as guaranteed by the 2nd Amendment, but I'm also for the responsibility to use them for defense, not to show someone what a bad-ass you are just because you carry one. In this context - Rights is only half a word; Responsibility is the other half.

I live in Texas and we are a concealed weapon state. Most cops will tell you that the majority of vehicles have a weapon in them, but I really don't see many public shootings. Compare that to Chicago, which has some of the toughest gun laws in the country, and that place is like a war zone. Now I understand that much of it is gang related, but other big cities have gangs, too. Chicago criminals know that the average citizen does not have a gun, so they take advantage of it. Pass all the laws you want, the bad guys will get their guns, period. I say that the rest of us need our guns to protect ourselves. That may be a terrible solution to some, but until they come up with something better, and practical, I see no choice.

I also think that we should put an armed guard in every school in America until the slaughter of innocent school children stops. Don't arm the teachers, put a roving guard in there who can be contacted by radio by any teacher or staff. Someone with the training and the willingness to shoot-to-kill when required. And stop broadcasting the names of those nutcases who do manage to kill people. I think other mentally unbalanced people see the notoriety the shooters get and want to know that they will be immortalized too, even if it means they must die doing it. Let's face it, most of these losers don't have much of a life anyway, so what are they really giving up?

But in all these cases, tragic as they are, it is not the GUN that is the problem. It always amazes me how some people always try to focus on the weapon and not the criminal.

Remember 9/11 when four airliners were hijacked? The weapon of choice was BOXCUTTERS ! Where is the outcry to ban all boxcutters?

13. The USA vs The World

I'm a baby boomer, born in 1946, right after WW II, which was our last legally declared war and the last war we ever won. At any rate, at the end of the war, the USA was king. Europe was in ruins, Germany was defeated, Berlin split in two, Italy came over to our side late in the war and Japan was Atomic Bombed into oblivion. Russia was on the winning side but much of it was destroyed. The war was fought in everyone else's backyard, Pearl Harbor being the exception. So when it was all over, we were the undisputed Military & Industrial Giant of the World. Not a bad position to be in, frankly.

Fast forward to 2014, but prepare yourself for a rude awakening.

We may still have the most powerful Military in the world, but that's like having a real big gun and not be willing to pull the trigger. What good is it if your enemies know damn well, that you won't pull the trigger? No, I am not a War Monger, but I realize that many other countries in the world hate our guts and would love to see us taken down a few pegs, if not destroyed altogether. So when we react to critical world events with nothing more than sword rattling and rhetoric, other countries just snicker and kick sand in our face. Most of the world knows just how weak and naive our president really is.

But I don't want you to get the wrong idea, so let me explain something. If I had a magic wand, I would gladly wave it and make all the hate, jealously and weapons of mass destruction in the world disappear. Poof, gone. I'd also make all the national leaders of the world get into the same room and not come out until they ALL agreed on world peace from that day forward. Sounds good, eh?

Well, I have no such magic wand, nor does anyone else. What we do have is a world in which there is hate, violence and the inescapable truth that as long as there are at least two people in the world, there will be war. It's the human condition, as they say. Yea, I know what the argument is; why can't those two people just talk things out and make peace? Well, because those original two people were Cain & Abel. That's right, the two sons of Adam and Eve. They were the first two people ever born and when they grew up, Cain killed Abel. That set the stage. If the only two brothers in the world couldn't get along, what chance do the rest of us have?

And history has proven that point ever since. People kill other people for a variety of reasons, but generally it's because one person has something that the other person wants. It's that simple. One person might want the food the other person has. Or they want the woman, or the gold, or the power or the land. Pick a reason, the result is the same. So countries do the same thing. One country wants something that the other country has. Now you can argue about the immorality of that, but you really can't argue against the historical facts.

So what should the USA do in this modern world? First, of course, is to protect ourselves. That is, by far, our primary responsibility. And we did a pretty good job of that, post WW II. Now by protection, I mean militarily, economically, culturally and, get ready, spiritually. I can hear the fireworks go off already. Separation of Church and State ! Yea, I know. By the way, did you know that that phrase, as often as it is quoted, never appears in the constitution? That's true. It does say that the government shall not establish a state religion, but it never says that the people can not establish their own religion. In fact, the First Amendment guarantees freedom of religion. So how the hell did we get to the point where we can't even say Merry Christmas without being politically incorrect? Just makes no sense at all. But I digress.

After we establish our primary responsibility of self-protection, then we need to re-establish our place in the world that we had a few generations ago. Now this may sound militant, but it's realistic. We let the world know, not just by rhetoric, but by our actions, that we will not put up ANY country trying to do us harm. That does not mean that we become the world's policeman, but it does mean that if our Embassies are attacked, someone will pay a very dear price. If you kidnap our citizens, be prepared to suffer the consequences. As I've said before, if there are no consequences, behavior will never change. Make the cost of those hostile actions high enough to make our enemies think twice. Will it be bloody? Yes, it will. But the other choice is to continue to let 3rd world piss-ant countries snip at us whenever they want. Now that's the stick, and it should be a big stick and we need to have the guts to use it.

We should also have a carrot. Not the wasteful "Foreign Aid" giveaway program that we have now, but a system based on other countries wanting to improve themselves with the help of our military and technical expertise. However, if any country refuses to help itself and wants to depend on the US forever, we cut them loose and let them go it alone.

Realistically this will take awhile, but countries will finally get the message that the USA in no longer going to be a Patsy, nor will we continue to throw money at some country just so they won't attack us. Nonsense.

Like it or not, there will be a natural pecking order among human beings. The question for us is, where on that pecking order do we want the USA to be.

But in the last few years, we have become weaker and weaker on the world stage.

Our friends should be loyal to us and our enemies should fear us. Neither of those things happen anymore. So we are left with a "Paper Tiger" image around the world and that is a very dangerous position to be in. We are not using our strength and that is just plain stupid. We bow down to foreign leaders and we throw money at other countries without it buying us anything. It just makes no common sense !

14. Common Sense

OK, I'm old fashioned, but let's take a shot at this. Long before Political Correctness invaded our culture, Good 'Ol Fashioned Horse Sense prevailed. I guess the term Horse Sense comes from the belief that even a horse is sensible enough to determine the difference between sense and nonsense. And certainly most people could too, back in the day. Then we got a little too sophisticated for our own good and we started to second guess ourselves. We worried about being sued, and with some justification, too. We allowed our TORT (Civil) Cases to get so carried away with huge judgments that just didn't make sense. Tort lawyers were in high demand, taking cases on speculation, betting on the fact that corporations would sooner pay out a few million, rather than face the bad publicity, regardless of the merits of the case. So more and more corporations caved under and paid out ludicrous amounts of money. Well, that started the avalanche and the general public knew a cash cow when it saw one. Common sense took a back seat and huge monetary judgments stepped to the front. Some of that still goes on today, but we are at least trying to get a handle on it. I will say that Texas has passed some significant TORT Reform Laws, for the better. Now, I fully understand that some of those people had a legitimate claim. I'm sure many did. But many of the awards from juries were just outrageous for the damage that was done by the entity being sued. True, some awards were lowered on appeal, but were still huge. So that is one place where common sense was attacked.

Here's another one. For God's sake, why is half the world running around just hoping to be Offended by the other half? You hear it all the time. Students or workers want to plan some event, or put up a sign concerning their own private business. But someone, invariably, will jump up and claim to be Offended. "Oh yes, I am Offended by that event or the sign you made. How dare you?" And quite often, the people who are Offended are not even from the area. They are people with nothing better to do than look around for any excuse to protest. Well, once that magic word is uttered, the whole world must stop and placate the Offendee. And the Offender must be severely chastised, preferably in public, or in court, and then beg for forgiveness. With God's blessing, and a few million bucks, the Offendee allows the rest of us to continue our lives, maybe. What Crap !! People running scared, not wanting to Offend anyone. How about instead of that we say something like; "If my sign Offends you, don't look at it !!

If the meeting we are holding Offends you, leave."

And if displaying the American flag Offends you or insults your religion or makes you feels uncomfortable, in any way at all........ Then I strongly suggest you leave the country and go back to wherever the hell you came from. End of problem.

Another is in matters of race. Now I addressed this subject earlier, but it flows into common sense, too. We worry about how we will be perceived. Will other people think we were prejudiced? OMG, what about the dreaded R word? Will we be called a Racist? Instead of blackmailing corporations for huge settlements, the media intimidates people with the threat of being called a racist. And we all know what happens then. You might as well wear a big R on your chest because from that point on, you are a pariah, to be vilified like the no good bastard racist that you are. Well, only if you are a white conservative, that is. If you are a black or white liberal, you can say pretty much anything you want or be as racist as you want and it's just fine.

So why does that exist, anyway? A shift in culture, I guess. With respect to lawsuits, at one time, there were manufacturers that took advantage of people. Many people were hurt or killed and that was unacceptable, so we changed things for the better by forcing companies to put out a safer product. But when the pendulum starts to swing the other way, it never stops at mid-point, it always swings to the other extreme. So the savvy and/or crooked people took advantage of the situation and made gobs of money at our expense. That's right, our expense. For one thing, the cost of goods and services keeps going up to pay for all those lawsuits. For another, regulation after regulation chokes off the ability to do business, and that is reflected in prices, too. In addition, insurance rates go through the roof and the consumer pays. It's always the consumer that pays. Now, some government oversight is a good thing. We need to have our food inspected and our medicine needs to be safe. But do we really need to have warning labels on plastic bags that tell us not to wrap this product around someone's head? Do we really need a warning label on bleach which tells us not to take this product internally? Or to be told not to eat razor blades? If you are not smart enough to know that, you should be institutionalized immediately, if not sooner. Besides, if you are dumb enough to do those things, you probably can't read anyway. In any case, stupidity should not be grounds for a lawsuit. I just read this and it's great:

Common Sense is a Flower that Doesn't Grow in Everyone's Garden.

With respect to the hammer of racism being banged on our heads, it probably stems from White Guilt which comes from our history of slavery. Now, as far as I know, no living white person in the USA has ever owned a slave, but that doesn't stop the guilt trips that are put upon us by those who would take advantage. True, slavery was the order of the day up until the Civil War, and racial problems continued long after the war with Jim Crow Laws, Segregation, Real Racism, etc. No question about it. For the record, black men owned slaves, too. Did you know that? Most people never heard of that and the black community isn't about to tell you. But it's true. Now, one more thing. In some isolated cases, there were actually black men who owned white slaves. Look it up, I did. Also many black men were part of the 'hunting parties' who captured black slaves in Africa for shipment back to the US and the Caribbean.

Now I am certainly not trying to say that things were equal all the way around. No, white men, for the most part, owned black slaves and although the treatment varied from owner to owner, none of it was good. Human Slavery, by definition, is sub human treatment.

By the way, read up on slave ships sometime. The mortality rate for the slaves on an ocean crossing could be as high as 50%, but the profit margin was so high, no one cared. Even for those who survived, the conditions were absolutely horrible.

But even though slavery is long gone, as are most of the segregation laws, many white people still suffer from the guilt hangover. Some of this comes from some members of the liberal media constantly stirring the pot and reminding us of how badly we treated black people. You know, if you constantly regurgitate an issue, you can never move on. If you purposely pick at a scab, it never heals.

So if you force people to feel this guilt, then you can push for all sorts of things in order to "make up for the terrible crimes you white people committed against us black people". Even though none of us were even alive back then, that doesn't matter. As part of their ignorance and/or manipulation, the Liberals always want to give black people more and more. We need to help these poor people and if you don't agree, well, you know what that makes you, right? Now here's the part that will really get some people upset, if they are not already there. When you treat any group of people as if they need extra help, they will always need extra help. If you feel this inner guilt and feel sorry for people and treat them like they are helpless and need extra care, money and attention, etc., some of them will take advantage and bleed you dry. But many will accept the very role in which they are portrayed; helpless, needy and generally unable to support themselves. That is not far fetched. People tend to act the way you treat them. Did you ever play the old trick on someone by having several people throughout the day tell a person that they don't look so good? People randomly make the remark that so and so looks pale or tired, etc. It's amazing how often people will actually develop the symptoms that they hear. Dependency is a disease, too. Sometimes you get it from people treating you that way.

Case in point: after Hurricane Katrina, I was watching a news report from New Orleans and there was a woman who was standing in water, maybe ankle deep, if that. She was in the middle of the street and the water was flowing, but not very fast and she certainly was in no danger whatsoever. But the TV camera was there and she was playing the part to the hilt. She looked helplessly into the camera and was crying for someone to help her. "Help me, Help me": Well, just to one side of the camera shot was a guy standing on the sidewalk and when he saw what was going on, he yelled to the woman, "Lady, just walk out of the water". Wrong thing to say. This woman was not happy. She just glared at him for a few seconds and then returned to the camera to play the victim, again. But the moment was lost, for her. It was priceless.

One other Katrina Story. Another woman was asking for help with food and a place to live, etc., also in front of the camera. This was the time when FEMA Trailers were all over the place. Then in the middle of her plea, she kind of caught herself, on camera, and said, "But I don't want a trailer, I need an apartment". Of course you do. Are you sure that's good enough, how about a penthouse and a new car?

Now, I am not minimizing the damage and deaths during Katrina. It was a real tragedy as I saw first hand when I worked in that area a few years later. I talked to people, black and white, who lost everything they had. But it is also not the full story. According to the media, New Orleans was ground zero for the storm and that is just not true. New Orleans got hit hard, sure, but areas to the east of it were wiped off the map. And a lot of the damage in New Orleans was from the dikes breaking, not the storm. The dikes broke largely because the money budgeted to maintain them had been diverted elsewhere. Ever heard that on any of the main street media outlets? How about this? It was all George W. Bush's fault because he hates black people. Yea, that's pretty much the way the liberal media reported it. And our good friend, Ray Nagin, Former Democratic Mayor of New Orleans, was right in the middle of it all. Yes, the same Ray Nagin who just got convicted of crimes committed during and after Katrina. Heard that in the news?

So, you take an overly litigious society, the stamp of racist freely applied to just about anyone, and wrap them both in a blanket of Political Correctness and guess what you have. A Mess. You have a society that is frozen by it's own fear of saying or doing something wrong and companies that are hesitant to introduce new products. Politicians have learned not to offend the wrong demographic, so they are even more wishy-washy than usual. People are slowly losing their right of free speech, partly because they are afraid to use it. And a government, which has completely lost whatever common sense it ever had, is taking bigger and bigger chunks of our freedom away, all under the guise of "helping us to be better, helping the poor to participate in society and helping our children to learn better".

Bullshit. And the national debt continues to climb, ever higher and higher.

So I just wonder sometimes. Where the hell is our National Common Sense? And if there is no end in sight, if there is no national call for sanity, where are we going from here? I wish I knew. Actually, I'm afraid I do know and so do you.

And that is why I COULD JUST SCREAM !!